TOURISM INDUSTRY IN INDIA.

Tourism in India has grown swiftly from the last few years and is turned to grow at faster speed in the upcoming years by the support of Indian government, the firm growth in the income, employment, development of infrastructure, international sports proceedings and Government of India's 'Incredible India' campaign launched in 2002 has also been quite successful. In order to hold dominance standards and services, the Ministry of Tourism approves travel agents, tour operators, and adventure tour operators in the country to a solid plan. As per the estimate of Ministry of Tourism, there are approximately 8,000 travel trade companies and firms including of tour operators, travel agents and tourist transporters. Tourist mostly visits the northern states of India where tourist flow grows 10.2% during 2014-2016 compared to the national average growth rate of 16.3 % during the same time frame. United States America and United Kingdom has the maximum number of foreign tourist visiting the northern states of Indian during 2016. Tourists were received from non-English speaking countries like Germany, UAE, Russia, and Japan etc. While tourists visit states of Punjab, Haryana and Delhi for business purposes, states of Himachal Pradesh, Uttarakhand, Jammu and Kashmir, Rajasthan and Punjab are chosen as relief and relax tourist spots. For religious tourism, they opt states of Rajasthan, Uttar Pradesh, Uttarakhand and Jammu and Kashmir. While multiple tourism circuits based on miscellaneous themes exist across northern states, in these areas the low level of stay durations by both domestic and international tourists indicates the need for more entertainment and leisure activities. India provides a wide collection of adventure sports for tourists. Trekking, Different water sports in Goa and scuba diving in Lakshadweep and Andaman & Nicobar, skating and skiing in the Himalayas, white water rafting and the camel and jeep safaris in the deserts, paragliding in Himachal, are just some of the options available for adventure tourists Buddhist circuit – There are various popular Buddhist tourist places in India, such as, Kushinagar, Rajgir,

Nalanda, Patna, Bodhgaya Vaishali, Sarnath, etc. these circuits attracts large tourists round the year. Religious tourism – India has a congregation of religious places stretching from Kashmir to Kanyakumari. Some of the important places include Madurai, Rameswaram, Tirupati, Varnasi, Dwaraka, Amarnath, Badrinath and Kedarnath, the tourist organization of India had its foundation from the year 1945. A committee was appointed in 1945 under the Chairmanship of Sir John Sargent, Educational Advisor, to the Government of India. The Sargent Committee submitted their provisional report in October 1946, but application of the suggestions given by this committee was implemented after 1947. As per the report of Sargent Committee, Tourist Traffic Committee was drafted in 1948. On the suggestion a Tourist Traffic Branch was created in 1949 with regional offices at Kolkata and Chennai. The tourist traffic branch was further promoted in 1955-56 from one branch to four branches and hand over a function to them via. Tourist Traffic, Tourist Administration, Tourist Advertisements, Distribution Section. The main elements of culture which attract tourist to a particular tourist spot fall under following categories: Pleasure climate, Adventure, Scenic attraction, chronological & cultural attraction, convenience, Shopping, Variety of cuisines, Accommodation, Relaxation & recreation etc. The travel and tourism industry has emerged as one of the best ever growing sectors contributing drastically to entire economic growth and development. While usually Europe and America have remained on the top in tourism markets, new promising markets are expected to witness high growth in international tourist visits over the next few years. India has noteworthy potential to become a preferred tourist destination worldwide. Its rich and diverse cultural heritage, rich natural resources and biodiversity provides abundant tourist attractions. Total tourist visits in various states of India over a five-year period reveal that while states of Karnataka, Delhi, Punjab, Chhattisgarh, Tamil Nadu and Jammu & Kashmir have improved their positions in 2016 as compared to 2002, those of Uttar Pradesh, Rajasthan, Uttarakhand, West Bengal, Himachal Pradesh and Kerala have witnessed a turn down. Key reason to the success of tourism in states is the increase in state investments towards the tourism sector. While the key business and leisure destinations of Delhi and Maharashtra get pleasure from good quality transport and accommodation infrastructure, states of Jammu & Kashmir, Uttarakhand, Himachal Pradesh, Rajasthan and Jharkhand may need significant improvements in their railway, roads and airport infrastructure.

The travel and tourism sector holds premeditated importance in the Indian economy providing several socio economic settlements. Provision of employment, income and foreign exchange, development or growth of other industries such as agriculture, construction, handicrafts etc, is some of the important economic benefits provided by the tourism industry. Investments in infrastructural facilities such as transportation, accommodation and other tourism related services and activities leads to an overall development of infrastructure in the economy. According to the World Economic Forum's Travel and Tourism Competitiveness Report 2017, India ranks 40th globally out of 140 economies ranked on world economic forum on Competitiveness Index slipped 1 place from 139 in 2016. India has been witnessing stable growth in its travel and tourism sector over the   past few years. Total tourist visits have increased at a rate of 16.3 % per annum from 577 million tourists in 2008 to 1057 million tourists in 2012 With the international tourist arrivals in India (pegged at 7.5 million in 2013) expected to witness an annual growth rate of 6.2 % over the next decade, visitor exports (expenditure generated by foreign tourists) are expected to amount to INR 2958 billion by 2023 growing at 9.6 % per annum. This growth can mainly be attributed to the rising income levels and changing lifestyles, diverse tourism offerings and policy & infrastructural support by the government such as simplification of visa procedures and tax holidays for hotels. India's splendid traditions and rich cultural heritage are closely related with the development of tourism. Its wonderful monuments attract a large number of tourists from all over the universe.

The natural surroundings, the architectural monuments, the music, dance, paintings, customs and languages all these go to make India as tourist glory.

Tourism is considered as a mechanism for economic activity since it offers marvelous potential in the field of employment generation and foreign earning capacity. Although tourism has occurred since Roman times, it has only become a major industry since the 19th Century. Increasing development of mass and resort tourism over the years has led to implication that the public is becoming dissatisfied with crowdie and air and water pollution and were searching for something new or different substitutes with the rise of alternative to get relax and relief. Tourism includes 'heritage tourism, ecotourism' 'educational tourism' Medical tourism, and other forms of tourism. Heritage tourism is an extensive category that embraces both eco-tourism and cultural tourism, with anxiety on conserving natural and cultural heritage. Heritage tourism is important for various reasons; it has an encouraging economic and social impact, it establishes and reinforces distinctiveness, it helps to preserve the cultural heritage, with culture as an instrument, it facilitates accord and understanding among people, it supports culture and helps refurbish tourism. In India, countless places are found that attracts the tourists. Example Kanyakumari attracts for sunrise and sunset, and strong and high Himalayas are world famous for mountain climbing. Seven monuments like Tajmahal, Kuthubminar, many more palaces are attracting the tourists. Tourism at present is very fast growing industry; it is also foremost growing industry, not only in India but also in the world. It has turn out to be an accepted global leisure activity. International Tourism demand continued to be robust between January and April 2015 with tourist arrivals increasing 4% worldwide according to the latest UNWTO World Tourism Barometer. Almost all regions enjoyed strong growth in tourist flow. Prospects for the May-August period remain upbeat, with close to 500 million tourists expected to travel abroad during these four months. European traders first came to Indian shores in 1498 with the arrival of European voyager, Vasco Da Gama. India was under the control of many different royal powers until the early eighteenth century when British rule fully came into place. The British remained in authority until 1947 when India became an independent nation. British control left a long-lasting impact on India, in many ways impeding India's development in some sector. After self-determination India developed in many different ways and develops enormously as compared to various developed countries. Earlier to sovereignty India was a country which was totally depend on agriculture.

After sovereignty this remained same, but with more support and modernisation and modern techniques now India ranks second worldwide in agricultural productivity. In recent times India has developed hastily in every segment. The rate of expansion in the services sector activity is expected to be continuous even in the next financial year as foreign tourist arrivals along with the number of telecom subscribers is set to boost. A major area of development in the countries services sector has been the tele-services and information technology sectors. After-independence, the Indian private sector began to expand with full potential. However, it faces foreign competition, including the hazard of cheaper Chinese imports. It has since handled the change by squeezing costs, revamping management, focusing on untrustworthy new products and relying on low labor costs and technology. Technology has been one of the main cornerstones of India's industrial development. The city of Bangalore known as the 'Silicon Valley' of India. Over 200 high-tech industries have been set up them including IBM, Intel and HP. These companies are part of India's growing IT sector while also being involved in software manufacturing. This expansion of IT and technology sector has stretch to most of India's other large cities such as Chennai, Mumbai and Kolkata and in 2015 the Information Technology sector contribute around 6.9% to GDP. Mining and other energy exploits have also been one of the main areas which have hard-pressed the industrialization of India since independence. India has the third largest coal reserves in the world and full-scale utilization of the coal resources began in the mid-1960s. India is developing very rapidly and is accepted by the whole world as one of the best developing country who has every reserve to become a developed nation very soon and is also considered as future super power.

DEFINITIONS OF TOURISM.

The Government of India through Tourism Department defines tourist as: "A foreign tourist is a person visiting India on a foreign passport, staying at least twenty-four hours in India and the purpose of whose journey can be classified under one of the following headings:

(i) Leisure (recreation, study, holidays, religion and sports).

(ii) Business, mission, meeting and health.

The definition of domestic tourist as given by the Department of Tourism Government of India is: "A person who travels within the country other than his usual place of residence and stays at hotels or other accommodation establishments run on commercial basis for duration of not less than twenty-four hours for any of the following purposes. Business, Study, Health, Pleasure, Pilgrimage. Tourism involves the activities of people travelling and staying in a place away from their home environment for leisure, business or other purposes.

In Sanskrit three terms of tourism have been derived from the word 'atana' that indicates going or leaving. This may be illustrated in the form of Paryatan-going out for pleasure and knowledge, Desatana –going out of the country primarily for economic gains and Tirthatana going out on pilgrimage.

Explaining the tourism industry is quite difficult. It is an industry that is not grouped into a particular title within the Standard Industrial Classification (SIC). The Explaining feature of tourism is not the manufactured product, but the 'tourist'. Most definitions focus on the services of a number of different industries such as the travel industry, hotels and catering, retailing and entertainment provided to tourists.

Mathieson and Wall (1982) define tourism as follows: "The temporary movement of people to destinations outside their usual places of work and residence, the activities undertaken during their stay in those destinations, and the facilities created to cater to their needs.

Saint Augustine defines tourism as "The World is a Book and Those Who Do Not Travel Read Only a Page.

Smith's (1988) observation, points out that though many tourism definitions meet the declared objectives, the substance of all definitions is weak. All of the definitions have not adequately reflected the business aspect of tourism.

Jafari (1977) the study of man away from his usual habitat, of the industry that responds to his needs and of the impacts that both he and the industry have on the host's socio cultural, economic and physical environments.

WTO 1981 Any person residing within a country, irrespective of nationality, travelling to a place within this country, other than his usual place of residence for a period of not less than 24 hours or one night for a purpose other than the exercise of a remunerated activity in the place visited. The motives for such travel may be.

1. Leisure (recreation, holidays, health, studies religion, sports)

2. Business, family, mission, meeting. (In smith 1988)

TOURISM IN INDIA- (AN OVERVIEW OF GLOBAL TOURISM SCENARIO).

The World Tourism Organization (WTO) is a supervisor evaluation organization to the United Nations (UN) and has the aim of promoting and developing tourism worldwide. It attempts to make possible world travel through eliminations or lessening of governmental measures for International travel as well as regularity of necessities for passports, visas etc. Each region of the world, Africa, Americas, East Asia and the Pacific, Europe, Middle East, and South Asia, receives special consideration from the WTO representatives. Travel and tourism have been a part of human life since the initial time and is at once linked with pleasures, adventures, productive experiences acknowledge. However, travel in the present set-up has become a profit-making intention. Tourism is the fastest growing industry globally and rebounded strongly, with international tourist arrivals grow up constantly. As a worldwide traded service, inbound tourism has become one of the world's major trade categories. The overall export income generated by inbound tourism, including passenger transport, exceeded US$ 1 trillion in 2010 and it closes to US$ 5 billion in 2016. Tourism exports account for as much as 30% of the world's exports of business services and 6% of overall exports of goods and services (WTO, 2011). Globally, tourism ranks fourth after fuels, chemicals and automotive products. For many developing countries it is one of the foremost sources of foreign exchange income and the number one export class, creating much needed employment and opportunities for development of income. Based on the presently split information from countries with data available, tourism's contribution to worldwide gross domestic product (GDP) is estimated at 5%. Tourism's contribution to employment tends to be somewhat higher and is estimated in the 6-7% in general number of jobs worldwide (direct and indirect). The contribution of tourism to GDP ranges from approximately 2% for countries where tourism is a relatively small sector, to over 10% for countries where tourism is an important stake of the economy (WTO, 2011). For islands and developing countries, or specific regional and local destinations where tourism is main economic sector, the importance of tourism tends to be even higher. In 2010, world tourism improved more strongly than expected from the hamper it suffered in late 2008 and 2009 as a result of the worldwide financial crisis and economic recession Worldwide. The majority of destinations reported encouraging and often double-digit increases, sufficient to offset losses or bring them close to this target. Recuperation came at different speeds – much sooner in most rising economies more than 8% and slower in most advanced ones with more than 5%. For 90% of countries in the world, tourism is one of the top four sources of foreign exchange. Caribbean countries obtain half their GDP from tourism. Tourism is the direct sources of foreign exchange that can help the country to preserve balance of payments and to compete at the world level to make their economy strong. India is the world's biggest tourism market with huge tourist flow of domestic as well as foreigners. India is more stable than its neighboring like Pakistan, Bangladesh, Iraq, Iran, Afghanistan and srilanka thus it receive more tourist from foreign countries then these countries.

TABLE NO 2.4. INTERNATIONAL TOURIST RECEIPTS IN BILLIONS.

YEARS	RECEIPTS IN BILLIONS US DOLLARS.	CHANGE (%)
2016	22.43	6.75
2015	21.01	10.17
2014	19.07	5.70
2013	18.04	0.39
2012	17.97	1.49
2011	17.71	22.22
2010	14.49	0000

Source: India, Ministry of Tourism, Annual Report 2015-16.

Interpretation: In India international receipts has grown from 22.4 billion Dollars in 2016 to 27.36 Billion dollars during last year. Contribution of tourism is constantly increasing as there is huge support of government for development of activities related tourism industry and political and social stability has been brought in by government that makes foreigners feel safe to tour India.

TOURISM DEVELOPMENT IN INDIA BEFORE AND AFTER INDEPENDENCE.

Tourism in India is economically very important and is growing quickly. Development of tourism has been given a high priority in the economic developmental programs of the country from the time 1980.In ancient India, there were no travel policy and regulations for travelling in the period of Chandragupta, and that time the famous Chinese pilgrim Fa Hien travelled to India in between A.D. 401 and 410 without a passport. But in the 3rd century passport or mudra became compulsory for all travelers. During this period tourist were accommodated at holy place of the country. There was an unpredicted boost in the traveler coming to India, as a result of the innovation of the new sea route by Vasco - de - Gama. When Alexander the Great reached in India, he found well maintained roads lined with trees and wells, and rest houses. Along with the imperial highway which is 1920 km long and 19 meters wide, men travelled in Chariots, palanquins, bullock- carts, on donkeys, horses, camels and elephants. During the British era, tourism in India becomes more intended. Dak Bungalows were built on the road side for the easiness of traveler. In Sanskrit literature the three famous words "Aththi Devo Bhava" means „the guest is truly god" are a dictum of hospitality in India. India is a storehouse of art, paintings; crafts appeared on pots found in the Indus valley civilization as early as the 3rd century. The British setup the India, a land of geographical diversity, sanctified with a rich civilization and culture. It is a potential tourism paradise with an wide-ranging variety of attractions ranging from beautiful beaches, hill stations, scenery, forts, monuments, fairs, festivals, art, crafts, culture, forest, wildlife, and religious centers etc. India has one of the world's richest natural heritage: 65,000 species of fauna counting 350 of mammals (7.6 % of the world's total), 408 of reptiles (6.2 %), 197 of amphibians (4.4 %), 1244 of birds (12.6 %), 2546 of fishes (11.7 %) and as well as 15000 species of flora (6 %) be a focus for the tourists for the development of tourism. India's forest, rivers, streams are satiated with affluent wildlife. In India, there are 80 national parks and 441 sanctuaries. The largest wildlife sanctuaries in Asia viz. Kanha National Park –Madhya Pradesh (Tiger project), Jim Corbett National Park

(Utter Pradesh) Gir (Gujarat) (Lion), Ranthambor (Rajasthan) (Peacock), Kaziranga (Assam) (Rihnosours), Bandipore (Karnataka) etc. The temples trail in India like Gurudwara in Amritsar, Tripati Balaji, Mathura, Ayodhya, Badrinath, Haridwara and Rishikesh. The hilly stations like Simla, Kulu, Manali, and Massoorie in the north, Shilling and Darjeeling in the east, Ooty, Kodaicanal, and Munnar in the south and Mahabaleshwar, Matheran, Chikaldara, and Amboli in the central. All these tourist destinations are mostly established, that create a center of attention large number of tourists. The tourist organization of India had its beginning from the year 1945. A committee was appointed in 1945 under the Chairmanship of Sir John Sargent, Educational Advisor of Government of India. The Sargent Committee submitted their provisional report in October 1946, the suggestions given by this committee was implemented after independence 1974. As per the report of Sargent Committee, Tourist Traffic Committee was appointed in 1948. On the recommendation a Tourist Traffic Branch was setup in 1949 with provincial offices at Kolkata and Chennai. The tourist traffic local office was supplementary extended in 1955-56 from one branch to four branches and hand over a function to them accordingly.

1) Tourist Traffic

2) Tourist Administration

3) Tourist Advertisements

4) Distribution Section

On March 1, 1958, a detach Department of Tourism was formed in place of a Tourist Traffic Branch under the Ministry of Transport and Communication which provides services such as accommodation, food facility, hospitality, etc One committee was appointed in March, 1963 under the Chairmanship of L. K. Jha. This Committee made quite a few recommendations to advance tourist flow in India, especially in regards to facilitation; three new corporations were setup in 1965, viz. Hotel Corporation, Indian Tourism and India Tourist Traffic Corporation but they did not work well and therefore amalgamated to make a single unit as India Tourism Development Corporation (ITDC) on October, 1966. ITDC is the chief organization of the Ministry of Tourism and Civil Aviation, which promoted tourism in India. Regional offices are located in every most important city in India. Besides, there are several other offices at essential point of international tourist interest. Tourist destination in the country are improved and provided more facilities to attract the foreign tourists. India is a land of great variety and contrast. Its solitary cultural air of mystery, exotic heritage, environment and outstanding natural resources has attracted international tourists. Mr. Pandit Jawaharlal Nehru, the first Prime Minister of Independent India, was the first person to notice the importance of tourism in the country. According to him, it was not only an appliance of earning foreign exchange but also a means of seeking international cooperation, understanding and peace between the nations. Tourism as an economic term in India was emerged only after Second Five Year Plan (1956). At the start going on a pilgrimage or visiting your acquaintances and relatives is what was meant to be Tourism in India. It was only after October 1966 when India Tourism Development Corporation (ITCD) was setup and India was promoted as a tourist destination not only for pilgrimage or visiting friends and relatives but as a holiday destination. The main important endeavor of ITDC was depiction proper consultancy services and promotes Tourism in India for developmental purpose. In 1982, the Indian Government allowed the National Tourism Policy which gave a six-point plan for Tourism development of Swagat, Suchana, Suvidha, Suraksha, Sahyog and Samrachana, meaning Welcome, Information, Facilitation, Safety, Cooperation and Infrastructure Development respectively. The main aim of this policy was to promote dispassionate socio-economic development, promote and preserve the rich heritage and culture of India and also create employment opportunities. Later on, Government of India initiated took several actions like the National Committee on Tourism was set up in 1988, setting up of the Tourism Finance Corporation in 1989 to finance tourism projects, the National Action Plan in 1992, the 1996 National Strategy for Promotion of Tourism and a new Tourism Policy in 1997 have all intended to promote the fast growth of Indian Tourism sector

UNIT NO.2

IMPORTANT TYPES OF NATIONAL AND INTERNATIONAL TOURISM IN INDIA.

All types of tourism in India have registered outstanding growth in the last decade. The Indian government decided to boost revenues from the tourism sector by projecting India as the fundamental tourist spot. The reason why India has been doing well in all types of tourism in India is that India has always been known for its hospitality, uniqueness, and attraction – attributes that have been attracting foreign travelers to India in lakhs every year. The Indian government, in order to boost tourism of a multiplicity of kinds in India, has set up the Ministry of Tourism and Culture. This ministry recently launched an operation called 'Incredible India' in order to encourage different types of tourism in India. the main elements that attract tourist to a particular destination fall under following categories: 1) Pleasure climate 2) Scenic attraction 3) Historical & cultural attraction 4) Accessibility 5) Shopping 6) Adventure 7) Variety of cuisines 8) Accommodation 9) Relaxation & recreation 10) Health - care projects. Therefore, it has been rightly said that the fundamental concept of tourism revolves around for 4 A‟s (a) Attraction (b) Accessibility (c) Amenities (d) Ancillary services.

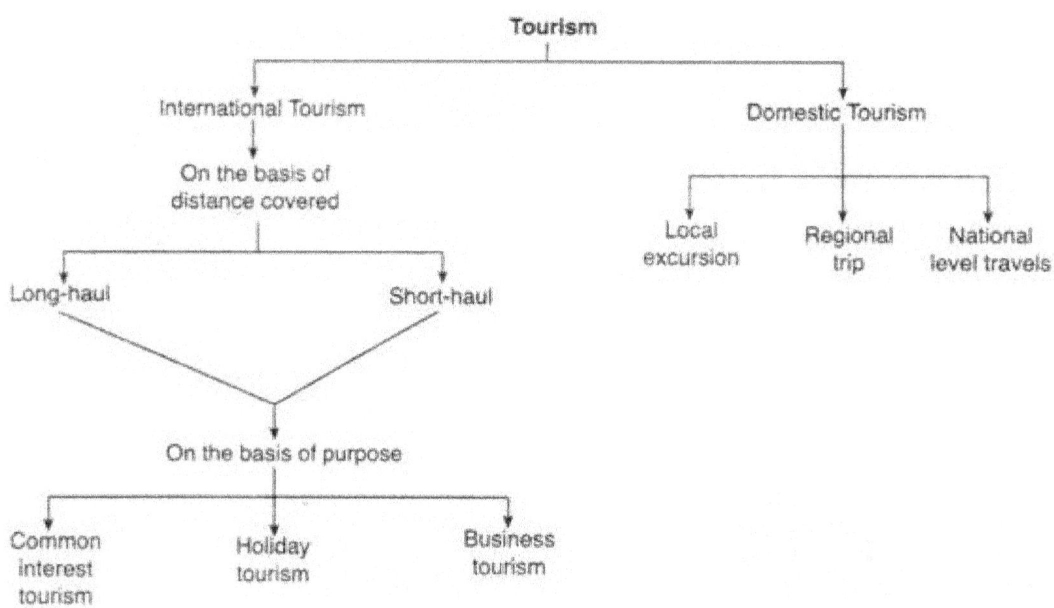

(I) International Tourism:

The globalisation of tourism, crossing borders, meeting different people, learning different culture and languages .it involves larger distance, from one country to another country. It plays important role in the economic development of any nation especially in developing countries international tourism plays important role in balance of payments, income and employment generations.

(ii) Domestic Tourism:

It consists travelling with in the controlled area. It is enclosed to certain limitations and involves peoples to travel with in the country are in state. It plays part in economic and employment generation of country. Domestic tourism consists local excursion, national level tours, etc.

(iii) Adventure Tourism

Adventure tourism involves ecstasy, excitement; high risk. high skill is required. It makes people to get knowledge about the new destinations, discover beauty and to know about unknown places. Parachuting, Hang Gliding, Bungee Jumping, water rafting, Rock climbing, Trekking, Mountaineering are the activities related to adventure tourism.

(iv) Alternative Tourism

Alternative tourism can be explained as 'forms of tourism that set out to be reliable with natural, social and community values and which allow both hosts and guests to enjoy positive and sensible interaction and shared experiences.' Therefore, eco-tourism can be understood to be one form of alternative tourism Eco-Tourism also known as ecological tourism is a form of tourism, which involves travel to destinations where flora, fauna and cultural heritage are the key attractions. Ecotourism is a conceptual experience, inspiring those who investigate into researching and understanding the environment around them. It gives us insight into our impacts, as human beings and also a greater appreciation of our own natural habitats.

(v) Educational Tourism

It is one of the swift growing tourism in world. It is developed because of growing population and technological outburst. It helps students, scholars, to learn about the environment technology and culture of other country to get knowledge and proficiency. Now a day's these tour is often carried out by colleges and universities.

(vi) Religious or Pilgrimage Tourism

A spiritual country where multiple religions are in extreme peace and harmony, India can rightly be called the 'Land of Faith'. Demonstration through the mighty mountains and one can experience godly presence. Religious tourism, also usually referred to as faith tourism; it is a form of tourism whereby people of faith travel individually or in groups for pilgrimage or leisure purposes. Sometimes, it is a journey or shrine of importance to a person's beliefs and faith. Members of many major religions participate in pilgrimages.

(vii)Sustainable Tourism

Sustainable tourism is envisaged as leading to management of all resources in such a way that economic, social and visual needs can be fulfilled while maintaining cultural integrity, essential ecological processes, bio diversity and life support systems." (World Tourism Organization) Sustainable development implies "meeting the needs of the present without compromising the ability of future generations to meet their own needs.

(viii) Wildlife Tourism

India has a rich forest cover which has some beautiful and unusual species of wildlife some of which that are even endangered and very rare. The places where a foreign tourist can go for wildlife tourism in India are the Sariska Wildlife Sanctuary, Kazi ranga National Park, and Corbett National Park. Wildlife sightseeing can be an eco and animal friendly tourism, usually presentation animals in their natural habitat. Wildlife tourism, in its simplest sense, is watching wild animals in their natural habitat.

(ix) Winter Tourism

Winter is one of the best seasons in India for travel and vacationing. Breath-taking beauty of Himalayan mountains, ample snowfall, panoramic natural views, frozen lakes, bonfire, winter festivals, adventure sports, and skiing facilities make India a popular winter destination for all sections of tourists with mottled flavors. Winter sports contribute to winter tourism. Many water sports holiday packages are available at places in many countries apart from Ski and Snow festival tours organized annually. Skiing is extremely popular in the mountainous areas. Ski festivals have variety of events like ski and sled competitions, ski and snow board lessons, performances and recreational activities. Majority of the event participants are from countries with a warm climate.

AN OVERVIEW OF INDIAN TOURISM SCHEMES.

The Ministry of tourism headed by the 'Union Minister for Tourism' is the nodal agency for the creation of national policies and programs allied to tourism. It also coordinates all the actions of the central government agencies, state government undertakings and the private sector for the development and promotion of tourism. The administrative head of the ministry is the secretary (tourism) who also acts as the Directorate General (DG) tourism. Directorate General of tourism has 20 offices contained by India and 13 offices in a foreign country. The work of the ministry is divided into 10 divisions which are headed by either a Director or Deputy Secretary level officer. These consist of administration, public sector undertakings (PSU) planning & coordination, division, promotion, international cooperation and actions divisions, market research division, abroad marketing division, hotels and restaurants division, travel & trade division, incorporated finance ,e-governance division, official language division, human resource development and domestic tourism division and parliament vigilance, administration & public grievances divisions. The first stirring and controlled efforts to promote tourism in India were made in 1945 when a committee was set up by the government under the chairmanship of Sir John Sargent, the then Educational Advisor to the government of India. Thereafter, the development of tourism was taken up in a premeditated way in 1956 coinciding with the second five year plan. The approach has evolved from isolated planning of single unit conveniences in the second and third five year plan. The sixth plan marked the beginning of a new era when tourism began to be considered as a major tool for social integration and economic development. But it was only after the 1980s that tourism activity gained momentum.

(i) Swadesh

Darshan Scheme.

The Union Ministry of Tourism had launched the Swadesh Darshan Scheme in 2014-15 with intend to develop theme based tourist circuits in the country. These tourist circuits will be developed on the ethics of high tourist value, competitiveness and sustainability in an incorporated manner. They will be developed by synergizing efforts to focus on concerns and needs of all stakeholders to improve tourist experience and increase employment opportunities. Under this scheme, 13 thematic circuits have been acknowledged for development. The five circuits identified under this Scheme are Buddhist Circuit, Himalayan Circuit, Coastal Circuit, Krishna Circuit and North-East Circuit. A Tourist Circuit is defined as a mean on which at least three major tourist destinations are located such that none of these are in the same town, village or city. At the same time, it would be ensured that they are not separated by a long distance. It should have well definite entry and exit points. A tourist who enters should get motivated to visit all the places identified in the circuit. The scheme is 100% centrally funded for the project mechanism undertaken for public funding. To leverage the voluntary funding available for Corporate Social accountability (CSR) initiatives of Central Public Sector Undertakings and corporate sector. financial support of individual project will vary from state to state and will be finalized on the basis of comprehensive project reports prepared by PMC (Programme Management Consultant). A National Steering Committee (NSC) will be constituted with Minister in charge of M/O Tourism as Chairman, to guide the mission objectives and vision of the scheme. A Mission Directorate headed by the Member Secretary, NSC as a nodal officer will help in recognition of projects in consultation with the States/ UTs governments.

Objective of Swadesh Darshan Scheme

1. Integrated development of Infrastructure in recognized theme based circuits.

2. Provide complete tourism experience with wide-ranging thematic circuits.

3. Follow community-based expansion and pro-poor tourism approach.

4. Creating alertness among the local communities about the importance of tourism for them in terms of increase in sources of income, improved living standards and overall development of the region.

5. Promote local arts, culture, handicrafts, cuisine, etc. to generate livelihoods in the acknowledged regions.

6. Tie together tourism potential for its direct and multiplier effects in employment generation and economic development.

LIST OF PROJECTS SANCTIONED UNDER SWADESH DARSHAN SCHEME.

S.No	State/UT	Name of Theme	Name of Project	Amount (Cr)
1	Andhra Pradesh	Coastal	Development of Kakinada Hope Island Konaseema as World class coastal & Eco Tourism Circuit in Andhra Pradesh	69.83
2	Arunachal Pradesh	North East	Development of Bhalukpong-Bomdila-Tawang in Arunachal Pradesh	49.77
3	Bihar	Buddhist Circuit	Construction of Cultural Centre adjacent to Maya Sarovar on the western side at Bodhgaya, Bihar.	33.17
4	Manipur	North East	Development of Tourist Circuit in Manipur: Imphal-Moirang-Khongjom-Moreh	89.66
5	Sikkim	North East	Development of Tourist Circuit linking - Rangpo (entry) (exit) in Sikkim	98.05
6	Uttarakhand	Eco Circuit	Integrated Development of Eco-Tourism,related Infrastructure of Tehri as New Destination-District Tehri, Uttarakhand	80.37
7	Andhra Pradesh	Coastal	Development of Coastal Tourism Circuit in Sri PottiSriramalu Nellore in Andhra Pradesh	60.38
8	Arunachal Pradesh	North East	Integrated Development of New Adventure Tourism in Arunachal Pradesh	97.14
9	Kerala	Eco Tourism	Development of Pathanamthitta-Thekkady as Eco Tourism Circuit in Idduki and Pahanamthitta Districts Kerala	99.22
10	Rajasthan	Desert Circuit	Development of Sambhar Lake Town and Other Destinations in Jaipur District, Rajasthan	63.96
11	Nagaland	Tribal Circuit	Development of Tribal Circuit Peren – Kohima-Wokha, Nagaland	97.36
12	Telangana	Eco Circuit	Integrated Development of Eco Tourism Circuit in Mahaboobnagar district, Telangana	91.62

13	Madhya Pradesh	Wild Life	Development of Wildlife Circuit at Panna-Mukundpur-Sanjay-Dubri-Bandhavgarh-Kanha-Mukki-Pench in MP.	92.22
14	Assam	Eco Tourism	Manas– Pobitora- Nameri- Kaziranga-DibruSaikhowa as Wild Life Circuit in Assam.	95.67
15	Mizoram	North East	Integrated Development of New Eco-Tourism at District Serchhip Mizoram.	94.91
16	Puducherry	Coastal	Development of Union Territory of Puducherry as Tourist Circuit	85.28

Ministry of Tourism, Govt of India 2014-16.

(ii) National Mission on Pilgrimage Rejuvenation and Spiritual Augmentation Drive (PRASAD).

This Scheme is planned to be implemented in a Mission Mode. The main Mission objectives and approach are as under: -

1. Integrated expansion of pilgrimage destinations in a planned, prioritized and sustainable manner to provide complete religious tourism experience;

2. Exploit pilgrimage tourism for its direct and multiplier effects on employment generation and economic development;

3. Follow community based expansion and pro-poor tourism perception in development of the pilgrimage destinations,

4. Striking the tourist attractiveness in a sustainable manner by developing world class infrastructure in the spiritual destination Promote local arts, cultural, handicrafts, cuisine etc. to generate.

These 13 cities have been identified for the development under the PRASAD Scheme:

Ajmer, Amritsar, Amravati, Dwarka, Gaya, Kamakhaya, Patna Kanchipuram, Kedarnath, Mathura, Puri, Varanasi and Vellankanni.

LIST OF PROJECTS SANCTIONED UNDER PRASAD SCHEME FOR YEAR 2014-16.

S.NO	NAME THE PROJECT	STATE	AMOUNT IN (CR)
1	Development of basic facilities at Vishnupad temple, Gaya, Bihar	Bihar	4.29
2	Development of Mathura-Vrindavan as Mega Tourist Circuit (Ph-II)	Uttar Pradesh	14.93
3	Construction of Tourist Facilitation Centre at Vrindavan, Distt. Mathura	Uttar Pradesh	9.36
4	Infrastructure Development at Puri, Shree JagannathDham-Ramachandi-Prachi	Odisha	50

Ministry of Tourism, Govt of India 2014-16.

TABLE NO 2.7. LIST OF PROJECTS SANCTIONED UNDER PRASAD SCHEME FOR YEAR 2015-16.

S.NO	NAME OF PROJECT	STATE	AMOUNT (CR)
1	Development of Karuna Sagar Valmiki Sthal at Amritsar	Punjab	6.45
2	Development of Amaravati Town, Guntur District of Andhra Pradesh as Tourist Destination	Andhra Pradesh	28.36
3	Development of Kamakhya Temple and Pilgrimage Destination in and aroundGuwahati.	Assam	33.98
4	Development at Patna Sahib	Bihar	41.54
5	Integrated Development of Pushkar/Ajmer	Rajasthan	40.44

Ministry of Tourism, Govt of India 2015-16.

(iii) E-Tourist Visa

The Government of India launched the e-Tourist Visa on 27.11.2014. During January-December, 2015 a total of 4, 45,300 tourists arrived on e-Tourist Visa. 150 countries are qualified for e-tourist visa as on 26.02.2016. This facility is now available in 16 airports as on 26.02.2016. The Government of India, w.e.f November, 2015, has also revised the e-Tourist Visa (e-TV) fee in four slabs of 0, US$ 25, US$ 48, and US$ 60. Right now e-TV application fee is US$ 60 and bank charge is US$ 2 which is uniform for all the countries. The revision of Visa fee has been done on the principle of reciprocity. Bank charges have also been condensed from US$ 2 to 2.5 % of the e-TV fee. There is no bank charge for zero visa fees.

(iv) Multi-Lingual Tourist Help Line

The Ministry of Tourism has launched the 24x7 Toll Free Multi-Lingual Tourist Help Line in 12 International Languages include Hindi and English on 08.02.2016. This service will be available on the accessible toll free number 1800111363 or on a short code 1363. This will be operational 24X 7 (all days) in a year offering a "multi-lingual helpdesk" in the chosen languages to provide support service in terms of providing information relating to Travel &

Tourism in India to the domestic and International tourists/visitors and to assist the callers with guidance on action to be taken during times of distress while travelling in India and if need be alert the concerned authorities. The languages handled by the contact centers include ten International languages besides English and Hindi, namely Arabic, French, German, Italian, Japanese, Korean, Chinese, Portuguese, Russian and Spanish. The calls made by tourists (both international and domestic) while in India will be without charge.

(v) Assistance to Central Agencies.

The objective is to make sure tourism infrastructure development through Central Financial Assistance of the Ministry by the Central agencies like Archaeological Survey of India, Port Trust of India, ITDC, Ministry of Railways, etc. who possess the assets. The Scheme for Infrastructure Development of Destinations and Circuits (PIDDC) has been delinked from the Union hold up from the current budgetary support for the scheme for the states; however, a provision of Rs. 20 crores has been made for the UTs only during 2015-16.

(vi) Training programs

A ten day's training programme has been launched to batter suitable tourism traits and knowledge amongst the trainees to enable them to work as Tourist Facilitators (PrayatakMitra). Young men and women so trained acts as channel/ resource persons in turn for similar effort. To steadily work towards a tourism-sensitive community for college going students including those enrolled with NCC & NSS in the age group of 18–28 years. This programme is implemented by IITTM. 59 candidates have been trained till January 31, 2016.

(vii) Incredible India Bed & Breakfast / Home stay Scheme.

The scheme offers foreign and domestic tourists an opportunity to stay with an Indian family and enjoy the affectionate hospitality and a taste of Indian culture and cuisine in a clean and affordable place. With a view to encourage the growth of such establishments and also to abridge the procedure of approvals, this Ministry has recently reviewed the guidelines by amending certain norms.

UNIT NO.3

GOVERNMENT CAMPAIGNS AND INITIATIVES TO DEVELOP TOURISM.

The government is well aware of the reality that it has to build infrastructure in order to improve the tourism sector. Therefore, it has expended more than half the selected budget on developing quality infrastructure at tourist destinations and circuits across the nation. The Ministry of Tourism has sanctioned 1,165 projects worth INR 38,726.7 million for tourism infrastructure development. The Indian government has played a decisive role in promoting the country as a brand in the global tourism market. Through its 'Incredible India' campaign, it has established the country as a destination with "something for everyone". The movement includes wide-ranging print, television and online advertisement campaign to augment the country's visibility on the international map.

MAJOR TOURISM PROMOTION CAMPAIGNS AND INITIATIVES.

Year	Particulars

1945	Sir John Sergeant Committee on Tourism
1947	Report of Sir John Committee
1949	Sir John Committee Suggestions,
1955	First Five Year Plan, No allotment for tourism development
1956	Allotment for tourism with name of transportation Division
1957	Establishment of Department of Tourism
1958	Establishment of Tourism Department Council
1960	Establishment of Indian Tourism Development Corporation (ITDC)
1963	L.K. Jha Committee Recommendations on tourism
1966	Establishment of Department of Aviation
1967	Establishment of Ministry of Tourism and civil Aviation
1968	Report on Cultural Tourism
1969	Estimates Committee of the Parliament on tourism
1970	Report of Indian Institute of Public Administration (IIPA) on tourism
1982	Declared First time Tourism Policy
1986	Establishment of National Committee and Separate Department Tourism
1988	Establishment of Ministry of civil Aviation Tourism
1991	Tourism as a source of Foreign Investment
1992	Nation action plan for tourism
1995	Establishment of Tourism cell
1988 /99	Tourism with export businesses
2000	Visit India Year
2002	The concept of highway tourism, agricultural tourism, and rural tourism A campaign titled as Incredible India was launched

2009	Another campaign titled as AthithiDevoBhava
2010	Hunar Se RozgarProgramme launched
2011	The Ministry launched its International TV Campaign 2010-11- Europe
2013	"Clean India" campaign launched
2014	Swadesh Darshan Scheme
2015	National Mission on Pilgrimage Rejuvenation and Spiritual Augmentation Drive

FUTURE OF TOURISM IN INDIA.

India's growing middle class and increasing disposable incomes has continued to maintain the expansion of domestic and foreign tourism. Domestic Tourist Visits to the States and Union Territories grow by 15.5 percent that is 1.65 billion provisional through 2016 with the top ten States and Union Territories contributing about 84.2 per cent to the total number of Domestic tourist visits, as per Ministry of Tourism. Foreign tourist arrivals in India increased 19.5 per cent year-on-year to 630,000 in May 2017. Foreign tourist arrivals on e-tourist visa enhanced 55.3 per cent year-on-year to 68,000 in May 2017. India's foreign exchange earnings through tourism improved by 32 per cent year-on-year to reach US$ 2.278 billion in April 2017, as per records from Ministry of Tourism, Government of India. India is expected to move up five spots to be ranked among the top five business travel market worldwide by 2030, as business travel spending in the country is likely to treble until 2030 from US$ 30 billion in

2015.International hotel chains will likely add to their growth and investment plans in India, and are expected to account for 50 per cent share in the Indian hospitality industry by 2022, from the current 44 per cent. The Indian tourism and hospitality industry has emerged as one of the key sources of expansion among the services sector in India. Tourism in India has significant prospective considering the rich cultural and historical heritage, variety in ecology, terrains and places of natural beauty stretch across the country. Tourism is also a prospectively huge employment generator besides being a notable source of foreign exchange for the country. The Indian government has realised the countries prospective in the tourism industry and has taken several steps to make India a universal tourism heart.

In the Union Budget 2017-18, the Government of India announced some initiatives to give a boost up to the tourism and hospitality sector such as setting up of five amazing tourism zones, special pilgrimage or tourism trains and worldwide launch of Incredible India campaign. The Ministry of Environment, Forest and Climate Change, Government of India, is scheduling to alter India's coastal regulation norms aimed at opening up the 7,500 km long coastline for developmental activities like tourism and real estate. The Central Government has taken a number of steps for soft transitioning to cashless mode of payment to ensure that no hardship is faced by the tourists and the tourism industry remains unaffected from government's demonetization move. India's travel and tourism industry has huge growth prospective. The tourism industry is also looking forward to the expansion of E-visa scheme which is expected to dual the tourist inflow to India. JW Marriott plans to have 175-200 hotels in India over the next four years. Accor Hotels India has adopted a born in France, made in India' approach to increase its properties in India, which has reached a total of 45 hotels and is, expected to increase to 55 hotels by 2017.

INCREDIBLE INDIA.

In 2002, India's Ministry of Tourism launched a campaign to promote India as a well-liked tourist destination. The slogan "Incredible India" was adopted as a slogan by the ministry. Before 2002, the Indian government on a regular basis formulated policies and prepared pamphlets and brochures for the promotion of tourism, however, it did not support tourism in a concentrated fashion. However, in 2002, the tourism ministry made a mindful effort to bring in more professionalism in its attempts to encourage tourism. It formulated an incorporated communication strategy with the aim of promoting India as a destination of choice for the perceptive traveler. The tourism ministry engaged the services of advertising and marketing firm Ogilvy & Mather (India) (O&M) to generate a new campaign to increase tourist inflows into the country. The campaign projected India as an attractive tourist destination by showcasing different segments of Indian culture and history like yoga, spirituality, etc. The campaign was conducted globally and received appreciation from tourism industry observers and travelers across the globe. However, the campaign also came in for disparagement from some quarters. Some observers felt that it had failed to cover up several aspects of India which would have been attractive to the standard tourist. In 2009, Minister of tourism, Kumari Selja revel plans to expand the Incredible India campaign to the domestic tourism sector as well. 12 million USD out of a total budget of USD 200 million was owed in 2009 for the purpose of promoting domestic tourism. In 2008, the Ministry of Tourism launched a campaign targeted at the confined population to educate them on the subject of good behavior and good manners when dealing with foreign tourists. Indian actor Aamir Khan was specially made to support the campaign which was titled 'Atithidevo Bhava', Sanskrit word meaning 'Guests are like God'. Atithidevo Bhava meant at creating wakefulness about the effects of tourism and sensitising the local population about protection of India's heritage, culture, cleanliness and hospitality. It also attempted to re-instill a sense of responsibility towards tourists and strengthen the confidence of foreign tourists towards India as a favorite holiday destination. The concept was designed to complement the 'Incredible India' Campaign. In 2015, Bollywood superstar Aamir Khan, whose comments on professed intolerance in the country had created a controversy, ceases to be the mascot for government's 'Incredible India' campaign as the contract for it has expired. "The contract was with the McCann Worldwide agency for 'Atithi Devo Bhava' campaign. The agency had hired Aamir for the job. Now the agreement with the agency is over. Ministry has not hired Aamir. Narendra Modi himself is the new brand ambassador of Incredible India. There is huge support of government in development of tourism and it is evident from the below table.

GOVT SUPPORT IN TOURISM DEVELOPMENT

RANK	Frequency	Percent	Valid Percent	Cumulative Percent
GOOD	68	13.4	13.4	13.4
V.GOOD	161	31.8	31.8	45.2
EXCELLENT	256	50.5	50.5	95.7
V.EXCELLENT	22	4.3	4.3	100.0
Total	507	100.0	100.0	

SELFSTUDY

INTERPRETATION: This describes the thinking of peoples that how much Government supports in tourism development as the question was asked to 507 respondents and out of which 256 i.e. 50.5% thinks that this government is working for better tourism while 31.1% are also in favor of this government by placing it at very good ranking for supporting tourism at 5 point ricter scale.

TOURISM INFRASTRUCTURE DEVELOPMENT

Expansion of excellence in tourism infrastructure all through the country is a key area of performance of the Ministry. Fifty percent of the Ministry's payments on Plan schemes are incurred for development of quality tourism infrastructure at various tourist places and circuits in the States and Union Territory. India has by now made a place on world's tourism map for the reason that of its great prospective to catch the attention of tourists to the miscellany of its tourist sites spread all over the country. It is also acknowledged that we still lay behind our other neighboring countries like China, Singapore, Malaysia and Thailand. An amount of Rs. 141.27 crore has been issued up to 31st December, 2015 by Ministry of Tourism for the North Eastern States during fiscal Year 2015-16 for expansion of infrastructure under recently launched schemes SWADESH DHARSHAN and PRASAD. For encouragement of fairs and festivals, an amount of Rs. 1.74 crore has also been approved to the North Eastern region. India is likely to grow at an average 9 percent per annum in next few years. Supplemented this expansion will be an amplify in demand for infrastructure services. Financial and inhabitant growth prospects are expected to place further pressure on active infrastructure facilities. In other words, a failure to respond to these necessities will cause halt to growth and obstruct poverty improvement efforts. The infrastructure investment has increased in the past few years, driven by government initiatives and private participation, but that need to be escalated in coming years.

TRANSPORT DEVELOPMENTS

A transport organization acts as a linkage between places of tourist origin and visiting places. It opens out an area by providing an access to its tourist places. In its absence, the resource potential for tourism i.e. attractions and amenities, can't be of any benefit. We cannot talk of the planning of tourism in an area without organising its transport system. The system consists of a set of connections of routes or means of transport and the modes of transport. The previous includes air, sea or water routes internal routes consist of roads or the motorways and the rail transport. The modes of transport refer to aircraft, ships, steamers, cars, taxies, luxury coaches, buses and the railway trains. Taxies, cars, motor like auto rickshaws, tangas, mopeds, bicycles and trams are particularly vital as items of local transport. It is supposed to carry travelers from airports, bus-stands or railway stations to hotels and tourist sites within a country. At high altitude places in tourist areas, you may come across ropeways and electric driven trollies, pony or tanga riding and sailing boats. Tourism is most eye-catching if a country has all realistic types of transport facilities both in its major and minor tourist destinations. Trunk routes are inter-state routes forming the countrywide network. They provide linkages among main transport hubs of India. The relations between the trunk routes and the nodal towns within a tourist region are mostly managed by local transport authority. It is a minor network at the regional level. Private travel organisations play a big role at the least possible level to look after the transport requirements of tourists within the nominal confined system.

AIR TRANSPORT

Airways are well-known to carry tourists over long distances. About 97% of international tourists arrive now a day in India by air. Within the country, 82% of them travel by air as compared to 11% by sea and water routes and 7% by land routes. Compared to 120 hours of sea travel, between London and New York in 1920, the up to date plane flying high above the zone of disturbing surface aircrafts winds takes 6 hours. These aircrafts typically fly at the speed of about 700 km per hour though these are capable to get the maximum speed of 1194 km per hour. These are clear to presume primary importance for universal tourism because of their enormous carrying capacity and high speed during nonstop flights. Discounted fares, in the form of concessions or easily manageable passes permissible for different age-groups, charged differently for off-season and the peak season, go a long way in the promotion of active tourism. High class travelers from wealthy countries coming additional as business tourists like to pay for costlier air travel even while moving about within India. The cause being that they want to complete their business deals and also visits to maximum tourist spots within the some degree of time at their discard. A beginning to better manage our air network has been made. It will convert 12 of our international airports into model ones and will upgrade the other ones at important tourist places.

SEA TRANSPORT

 It has lost its choice to air carriage of passengers over long or time intense distances. But for petite distances as from Mumbai to Goa in our coastal waters, in lakes like Chilka or Vembanad, hopping from mainland to islands or from one to another island holds promise for tourists. All comprehensive package tours for domestic and for the foreign tourists from Kochi to Lakshadweep islands and from chennai or Kolkata to Port Blair and Car Nicobar are becoming popular. Such a tour includes the total cost for providing travel accommodation and other facilities. In the long run, the improvement of direction-finding in suitable stretches of river like Brahmaputra in Assam could provide immense possibilities for opening out new route for tourist travelers.

ROAD OR MOTORWAYS

From early 1960s a larger use of private cars entirely for an wealthy individual and his family, and of taxies, luxury coaches, buses for lower budget group of 9 to 30 persons, have been gaining fame. The National highways and motels built along picturesque and full of activity roads have revolutionised their use by the holidays. Motorways provide shift and easy associations within the network of major routes. Motor transport comes ahead to carry passengers to less costly areas along the highways away from the jam-packed city hotels. This ready-at-hand facility reduces the uncontrollable crowds of visitors inside the great cities during busy period. It also provides a big relief to low budget tourists and the vacationing students. India is paying superior attention to accumulating new roads and improving the existing ones, for this reason. The construction of four to six lanes highways, stretching over 5952 km will be connecting our four most important metro cities in response to the fundamental demand of tourist traffic. A side suggestion is to complete two corridor roads connecting Srinagar and Kanyakumari from north to south and Silchar to Porbandar from east to west direction. These corridors will respectively extend to 4000 km and 3300 km.

RAIL TRANSPORT

Railway provide only the low budget comforts, while rail routes connected major cities within 200 to 500 km distances; one of the world's biggest railways is in India the very long distance sub continental service inclusive over several hundred kilometers. The most noteworthy trunk routes connecting different big cities like Mumbai, Chennai, Kolkata, and Delhi. A great north-south derivative rail route has now reached Jammu-Udhampur in Jammu and Kashmir (finally to be extended to Baramulla via Srinagar) state and Kannayakumari in Tamil Nadu at the end of country's mainland. Nearly all main rail routes have been electrified to make sure clean and quick travel. Metro rails are fast coming up in India's tiring metropolises as another tourist attraction. How rightly it is said that travelling India by train offer the places of interest, sounds and smells of stations as well as a variety of people, over a route length of more than 60,000 kms.

HELIPADS

Himachal Pradesh is one of the best places to visit and is developing with great velocity. Himachal Pradesh currently has 63 functioning helipads. The State Government is also constructing new helipads at Banderaru near Sanjauli and Chowari, District Chamba. In both the places the forest land is involved, thus it is taking time to get approval from Forest Conservation Agency. After receiving approval, further action will be taken.

SHIMLA AIRPORT

The work of widening of landing strip of Shimla Airport from 23 meters to 30 meters has been accomplished by the Airport Authority of India. Refueling service is also in advance phase of completion and is feasible to be functional as soon as commercial flights are resumed.

CRUISE TOURISM

A Task Force on Cruise Tourism was constituted on November 24, 2015 to aid develop the vast seashore of the country and promote cruise tourism. Government of Himachal Pradesh is very keen to develop the various different types of tourisms to attract lot of tourists to the state as it is considered as back bone of the economy of Himachal Pradesh.

GOLF TOURISM

To target high-end tourists and endorse golf tourism in India, eight golf events have been approved by India Golf Tourism Committee (IGTC) during the year 2015-16 (till December 2016) and Rs.281.71 lakh released for the same.

Transportation acts as a life link between places of sightseer origin and the place they are visiting. It provides an access to tourist places. The tourists chose diverse types of sources to travel. The below table provides the perfect look how and what type of moods of transportation has been used by tourists to reach Himachal Pradesh.

TOUR OPERATION AND MANAGEMENT

Tour Guides is the long run profitable activity, a tour guide induces the visitors to the attractions of a sightseer place or a tourist area and conducts them around the genuine tourist spots. At the lowest local level, tour guidance is the primary unit for encouragement of the whole programme of tourism. A successful tour guide needs to be adequately aware of the geography of the area, background of the localities of tourist interest, past history including legends about temples, shrines, monuments ruins of old sites and forts on the list of sightseeing. A good tour guide is anticipated to talk about the significant local traditions, culture, folk lore, performing arts, festivals and fairs for creation the unfolding into an appealing story for the tourists. The facts about the tourist sight must be told clearly in the introduction. Guide must be friendly He or she will better be speaking to the tourists in their language or the language they be aware of. An experienced guide is capable to know the viewpoint of tourists just on enquiring about the country from where they came.

Tour Operators

The operation of tourism has now become a job of expert nature. Now a day, it is becoming a tough task for any single functionary to look after all parts of the administration of tourism. The work of a tour operator for that concern is entirely different from that of a tour guide. A tour operator has the job of managing the transport requirements, visa and permit clearance official process and booking of hotel accommodation for the tourists. Such a person must go on updating the information about latest changes made normally in the concerned rules and regulations. A tour operator has to build up a operational relationship with the personnel managing the booking of transport and hotel reservations at or close to the tourist sites. He must also know from where to employ tents and other tools for an adventurous tourism. Now-a-days, a tour programme has to be decided much ahead of time. Those days are gone when one could start travelling anytime one wished for a business or leisure time tour. A group of tourists or even a single tourist has a pre-fixed plan for touring.

HOTELS & RESTAURANTS

Hotels are an important section of the tourism produce. They contribute to the overall tourism experience through the standard of facilities and services offered by them. With the aim of providing up to date standards of facilities and services available in the hotels, the Ministry of Tourism has formulated a voluntary scheme for classification of operational hotels which will be applicable to the following categories: Star Category Hotels: 5 Star Deluxe, 5 Star, 4 Star, 3 Star, 2 Star & 1 Star Heritage Category Hotels: Heritage Grand, Heritage Classic & Heritage Basic. Before World War second, most hotels in India were developed in locations that were often used by the British and Indian aristocracy. This period saw the development of hotels being undertaken by individual British and Indian entrepreneurs, with only a few companies owning hotels in India, such as The Taj Group--Indian Hotel Company owned by J. R. D. Tata and Faletti's Hotel, East India Hotel oberoi Group. The fundamental hotels that were built during India's British period were: The Rugby, Matheran (1876) The taj Mahal Hotel, Mumbai (1900) The Grand, Calcutta (1930) The Cecil Hotels, Shimla and Muree (1935) The Savoy, Mussoorie (1936) India got independence in 1947, and the hotel industry had a period in which number of hotel development took place. Late Pundit Jawaharlal Nehru, then Prime Minister of India, recognized that tourism could be an engine for the country's economic enlargement and was inspired to build worth hotels in India for visiting foreign dignitaries. This led to the first-ever government investment in the hotel industry with the building of the Ashoka Hotel in New Delhi. The India Tourism Development Corporation (ITDC) was set up in 1966 as a corporation under the Indian Companies Act of 1956, with the merger of Janpath Hotel India Ltd. and India Tourism Transport Undertaking Ltd. Today, ITDC provides a complete range of tourism services, including accommodation, catering, and entertainment and shopping, hotel consultancy, duty free shops, and an in-house travel agency. The government gave the tourism industry another augment when it created the Ministry of Tourism and Civil Aviation in 1967, separating it from the Ministry of Transport and Shipping, thereby recognizing that tourism was not merely about transporting people from one point to another but had a much wider role to play in the nation's economy. Concurrently, Rai Bahadur M. S. Oberoi, Chairman of East India Hotels Ltd., was expanding their empire by constructing New Delhi's first modern multi-story hotel, which was franchised to U.S.-based Inter-Continental Hotels. The portfolio of Oberoi hotels consisted of The Cecil, Shimla; The Oberoi Grand, Calcutta; The Oberoi Clarks, Shimla; The Oberoi Palm Beach; and Gopalpur on the Sea. The building of hotels is going well all over the country now a day

PROMOTIONAL ACTIVITIES

Advertisements and posters on Himachal Pradesh and Northern States were created for promoting of tourism. These advertisements were telecasted as part of North-East and himachal Pradesh Campaign shown on private channels and Doordarshan. The Ministry is devoted to the development and promotion of tourism in the North- Eastern Region and especially himachal Pradesh and all the hard work are made to ensure that these areas come out as the leading tourism places for domestic and foreign tourists in the countryside. The whole thing like printing of posters, brochures, banners etc. and release of advertisement are for boosting tourism. India is a country with a wide variety of tourist attractions and facilities. It however, gets exaggerated from the problems of economic under development including insufficient basic infrastructure, lack of hygiene, cleanliness in public places etc. On the other side there is fierce competition in tourist generating market from a number of nations for attracting a large number of the tourists to their countries. Thus special stress was put to strengthen its promotional and marketing efforts to uphold its active market as also to penetrate into new markets like Korea, South Africa, Israel, C.I.S Countries. Steps were taken to undertake Market Research and marketing segmentation analysis to know about tourism. The promotional efforts of the abroad field offices are to be supplemented and incorporated with the efforts of Indian Missions and other agencies abroad. Air India, Indian Airlines sales offices abroad also to enhance the efforts of the Ministry of Tourism. The specific elements of promotional efforts abroad to include:

- Advertising

- Printing of brochure in local languages

- Brochure support

- Joint advertising with Tour Operators/Travel Agents

- Promotion of Charters

- Production of promotional aids

- Festival of India

- Production of films and audio-visuals in local languages

- Trade Posters, Seminars/Tourism Talk Shows

- Direct mail and correspondence

- Participation in Tourism Trade Fairs.

MULTILINGUAL TOURIST HELPLINE

The government of India and The Ministry of Tourism launched the 24x7 Toll Free Multi-Lingual Tourist Helpline in 12 languages on February 8, 2016. It can be contacted on Toll Free Number 1800-11-1363 or short code 1363. The languages provided by the Tourist Helpline include ten global languages besides English and Hindi, namely, Arabic, French, German, Italian, Japanese, Korean, Chinese, Portuguese, Russian and Spanish. The multi-lingual help desk in the selected languages provides support service in terms of providing information involving to Travel and Tourism in India and help the callers with counsel on action to be taken during times of distress while travelling in India and if need be alert the concerned authorities. This is to make the tourist to feel safe and secure in our country.

TOURIST INFORMATION CENTERS

There is a map to network information centers with hotels & tour operators for room booking & tour planning. Information promotional material with tourism related information would also be available at the centers. Locally made products like juices, handicrafts, jellies, will also be available at these centers. At this time there is a lack of tourist information centers in the state. These centers need to function as marketing units to a tourist national as well as foreign who has entered the state.

E-TOURIST VISA

 The Government of India has come out with the e-Tourist Visa on 27.11.2014. During January- December, 2015 a total of 4, 45,300 tourists arrived on e-Tourist Visa. 150 countries have been made entitled for e-tourist visa as on 26.02.2016. This service is now available in 16 airports as on 26.02.2016. The Government of India, on November, 2015, has also revised the e-Tourist Visa fee in four slabs of 0, US$ 25, US$ 48, and US$ 60. At present e-TV application fee is US$ 60 and bank charge is US$ 2 which is the similar for all the countries. The revision of Visa fee has been done on the principle of reciprocity. Bank charges have also been condensed from US$ 2 to 2.5 % of the e-TV fee. There is no bank charge for zero visa fees.

SETTING UP OF NEW TOURISM EDUCATIONAL COLLEGES.

Institutes of Hotel Management:

A total of 42 Institutes of Hotel Management (IHMs), consisting of 21 Central IHMs and 21 State IHMs, and 9 Food Craft Institutes (FCIs), have come up with the hold up of the Ministry of Tourism. These institutes are set up as self-governing societies with specific mandate to impart hospitality education conduct education in hospitality skills. During the year 2015-16, standard agreement has been accorded for the setting up of three new State Institutes of Hotel Management (SIHMs) i.e., one each at Ramnagar (Uttarakhand), Jhalawar (Rajasthan) and Sawai Madhopur (Rajasthan) with the Central Financial support of Rs. 16.5 crores. The Ministry of Tourism till August 2016 has certified 12 Institutes of Hospitality Management in the North Eastern States. Thirty Out of these Central Institute of Hotel Management only few likes of Guwahati, Central Institute of Hotel Management, Shillong, State Institute of Hotel Management, Gangtokand Food Craft Institute, Nawgaon are operational.

Food Craft Institutes (FCI)

Government has accorded permit for setting up of Food Craft Institute at Khajurahoin Madhya Pradesh, and has sanctioned Central Financial aid of Rs.475.00 lakhs. During the year 2015-16, in-principle agreement has also been accorded for setting up of two Food Craft Institutes (FCI) at Dholpurand Baran(Rajasthan) with the Central Financial Assistance of Rs. 7.50 crores

Adventure activity training course

The tourism department is planning to carry out short adventure teaching courses for water sports at Govind Sagar and Maharana Pratap dam, for para gliding at Solang, Bilaspur & Bir in Kangra in 2016. The government, however, is not yet permissible to conduct such training courses. Staff training programme is an attempt to provide the visiting tourists a courteous, helpful and hospitable customer leaning scheme. The guides should be trained with detailed information about the area/city, awareness of sanitation and integrity. The front place of work training should be provided for fluency in English and motivate to be helpful. Apart from these, training should also be provided to:

• State tourist bus drivers on good manners and careful driving.
• Airline counters staff on effective communication on times of crisis.
• Hotel staff in reception, maintenance, room service.

COOPERATION WITH WORLDWIDE ORGANIZATIONS

international Co-operation Division is one of the important divisions of the Ministry of Tourism, which engages in a variety of consultations and negotiations with the international organisations such as United Nations World Tourism Organization (UNWTO); Economic and Social Commission for Asia and the Pacific (ESCAP); Bay of Bengal Initiative for Multi Sectoral Technical and Economic Co-operation (BIMSTEC); Mekong-Ganga Co-operation (MGC); Association of South East Asian Nations (ASEAN) and South Asian Association for Regional Co-operation (SAARC) and South Asian Sub-regional Economic Co-operation (SASEC). This dissection holds consultations and debate with other countries for signing of Agreements for bilateral/multilateral cooperation in the field of tourism, organizes mutual Working Group Meetings with other countries and attends cooperative Commission Meetings in coordination with the Ministries of Commerce, Culture, External Affairs, Civil Aviation, Finance, Petroleum, etc. for development and promotion of tourism.

Agreements Signed in the Field Of Tourism.

Agreement between the Government of India and the Government of the French Republic for reinforcement the collaboration in the field of tourism was signed on 09th April, 2015.

An accord between the Government of India and the Government of China for underpinning the cooperation in the field of tourism was signed during the State visit of the Prime Minster of India to China on 15th May, 2015.

1. The Government of India and the Government of the Republic of Uzbekistan signed an accord on cooperation in the field of tourism on 6th July, 2015 in Tashkent.

2. The Ministry of Tourism, Government of the Republic of India and The National Council of Tourism and Antiquities of the United Arab Emirates signed an agreement on cooperation in the support of tourism on 3rd September, 2015 in New Delhi.

3. The 5th Meeting of the SAARC Working Group on Tourism was hosted by the Ministry of Tourism, Government of India in New Delhi during 25-26 November, 2015, in the Chairmanship of Shri. Vinod Zutshi, Secretary, Ministry of Tourism, Government of India. The Indian delegation was led by Shri Suman Billa, Joint Secretary, Ministry of Tourism, and Government of India and comprises legislative body from Ministry of External Affairs, Ministry of Home Affairs, Ministry of Culture, Air India as well as stakeholders from the Tourism and Hospitality industries. The meeting was attended by all the stakeholders from all SAARC Countries. Dialogue was detained on Strategies/ Action Plan to encourage intra-regional tourism in the SAARC region as well as for endorsement of the SAARC region as a tourist places in international source market.

FACTORS AFFECTING TOURIST BEHAVIOUR

There are number of factors that enormously modify tourist behavior to visit any country or state, likewise himachal Pradesh is one of the world's best tourism place but the political unsteadiness makes people dread to visit heaven on earth hence the people related with this industry suffer huge loses every year.

Geographical Factors: Some physical factors like geological and climatic conditions, facilities and facilities available at the places, advertising and marketing conducted by tourism business alter the choice making of the tourists.

Social Factors: A few social factors such as a person's social set of connections, which provide first had information that can alter a person's decision of visiting or not visiting a particular place.

Place of Origin: There can be a extensive spectrum of tourist behavior depending upon the place they belong to. North Americans like to follow their own cultural framework. Japanese and Korean tourists like to visit places in groups.

Tourism places: It is a major causal factor altering tourist behavior. If a places has all basic provisions such as electricity, water, clean surroundings, proper accessibility, amenities, and has its own implication, it largely attracts tourists.

Education of Tourist: The more educated the tourist is the wider range of choices, curiosity, and the information of places he would have. This drives the decision making when it comes to choosing a places.

UNIT NO.4

HOSPITALITY

In today's fast pace world, the hospitality manager's need to be multi-talented & multitasked individuals. Besides, their domain knowledge of Hotel operations like Food & Beverage Production & Service, Room Division Operation's, Marketing, Revenue Management; they are required to assume specialized roles such as employee counselor, facility engineer or computer system analyst. In today's highly competitive & diverse business environment, the skill level required for success today in this field is greater than it was in the past. Hospitality Management has always been a very challenging & precision perfection profession. This is exhibited in their multi-faced roles like in a casino operation, 5-star hotel, Outdoor catering, In-flight catering & Industrial Catering operations. Day after day, in hundreds of situations, the action of operational mangers of Hotel's will influence the likelihood of the business or the manager becoming the subject of Litigation. Almost all the activities in Hotel operations & Tourism Industry is covered by legislation. Most of the legislation pertains to the start of Hotel operations & Tourism. but some of the aspects are complicated and need expert's advice time to time, so as to resolve the legal requirements.

The major thrust of Hotel and Tourism Laws are to govern & regulate the activities of the professionals, guests & other related entities. The laws provide an assurance of their professional competency &stability. In this process the professionals of Hotel & Tourism Industry acquire legal status by way of legislations. This legislations in turn clearly defines the professional'sroles in both the industry. It invariably means to cover tourism & hotel industry categories and activities like –

☐ The conditions imposed on each category

☐ The protection given

☐ Legal provisions of the acquirer's controls

☐ Illegal acts

☐ Loss of license

In order to keep the above categories & activities intact, the following legislations need to be enacted –

1) Laws that will regulate the professional status of Travel & Tourism Industry

2) Laws that govern the professionalism of tourist guides

3) Laws that will govern the professional status of

a. Hotels,Resorts,

b. Food & Beverage establishments like – Bar,Pubs,Restaurants, Fine

Dining,Snack-bars,Fast-food outlets

c. MICE Companies (Meeting,Incentive, Conference & Exhibition

Companies)

Hospitality –Definition- (OxfordDictionary) Hospitality is defined as: _Reception and

Entertainment of guest, visitors or strangers with liberality and goodwill. _

Hotels - Definition - An establishment whose primary business is providing lodging Facilities for the general public and which furnishes one or more of the following services.

☐ Housekeeping service

☐ Food and beverage service

☐ Bell and door attendant service

☐ Laundry and dry cleaning

☐ Concierge

☐ Use of furniture and fixtures

HOTEL CORE AREAS - Revenue Earning Department

Front Office Department- It is Responsible for Welcoming & registering the guest, allotting rooms& Helping guest check outs.It is headed by Front Office

Manager

Housekeeping Department- It is responsible for cleanliness & upkeep of front of the house areas as well as the back of house areas. This department is headed by

Executive Housekeeper.

Food & Beverage Service Department- It constitutes the Restaurants, Bars, Coffee Shop, banquets & Room Service. This department is headed by Food &

Beverage Manager.

Food Production Department- It constitutes the Kitchen & Bakery. This department is headed by Executive Chef.

HOTEL SUPPORT AREAS

Maintenance Department- This department is responsible for all kinds of maintenance, repair and engineering work on equipment's, machines, fixtures, and fittings.

Human Resource Department- Recruitments, Orientation, training, employee

welfare, compensation, labor laws & safety norms of the hotel are under preview of Human Resource Department. This department is headed by Human Resource

Manager.

Sales & Marketing Department- The function of this department is 5-fold – Sales, personal relations, and advertising, getting MICE. This department is headed by

Sales & Marketing Manager.

Financial Control Department- Inventory control procedures are the responsibility of this department. This department is headed by Financial

Controller.

Security Department- This department is responsible for safeguarding the assets, guests and employees of the Hotel. This department is headed by Chief Security

Officer.

Purchase Department- The procurement of all departmental inventories is the responsibility of purchase department. This department is headed by Purchase Manager.